D0598167

A Child's First Library of Learning

Dinosaurs

TIME-LIFE BOOKS • ALEXANDRIA, VIRGINIA

Contents

What Were Dinosaurs?

(ANSWER) Dinosaurs roamed the earth millions of years ago. They lived and died out long before people came along. Dinosaurs were like a group of animals that are still living today. These animals are called reptiles. Snakes, lizards and crocodiles are all reptiles.

Dinosaurs, snakes and crocodiles: all reptiles.

■ How were they alike?

Dinosaurs laid hard-shelled eggs like those of snakes and other reptiles.

They had the same dry, scaly skin that snakes and lizards have today.

Their bodies were as cold or hot as the temperature around them.

■ How were they different?

Dinosaurs walked in a different way than reptiles. Most reptiles crawl or waddle because their legs stick out from the sides of their body. Dinosaurs' legs were right under their bodies, so they could walk on four feet and stand like mammals. A great number of them, including the vicious Tyrannosaurus rex, could stand on two feet.

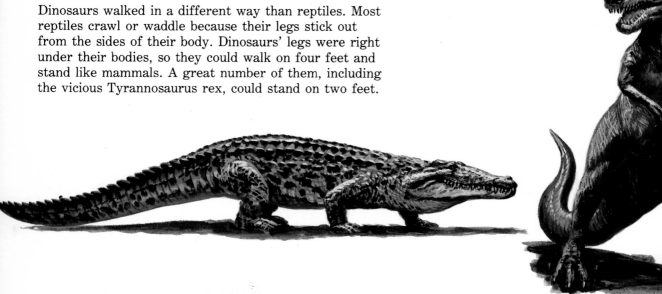

What Do Dinosaur Skeletons Show Us?

We can use their skeletons to split dinosaurs into two main groups. One group is the saurischians. The other group is the ornithischians.

Tyrannosaurus, a saurischian

Stegosaurus, an ornithischian

Were dinosaurs the only creatures living in their time?

Among the other animals that lived when dinosaurs did were some that could fly and some that could swim. They were all reptiles. Flying reptiles included the great winged pterosaurs. Among the sea reptiles were nothosaurs, mosasaurs, ichthyosaurs and plesiosaurs.

Nothosaurus

Rhamphorhynchus

● **To the Parent**

While dinosaurs exhibit a number of reptilian characteristics they actually belong to a group called archosaurs. This group includes the modern crocodile as well as the now-extinct thecodonts and pterosaurs. Their distinguishing features were the bone structure of their legs, which fully supported their bodies from beneath; and hip joints, which enabled them to walk and run straight and fast, whether they were on two feet or moving around on all four.

5

How Long Ago Did Dinosaurs Live?

ANSWER Dinosaurs first appeared on earth about 225 million years ago. They grew and changed as our planet developed. About 65 million years ago the last of the dinosaurs died out.
You can follow the growth and development of the dinosaurs in the drawings on these pages.

In the Carboniferous Period trees appeared. Froglike animals were the first creatures to crawl onto land.

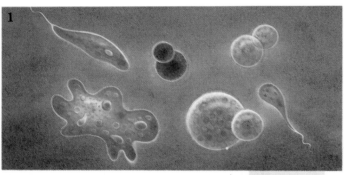

The earth began to form about 4.6 billion years ago. Life forms began to appear about 3.1 billion years ago.

Animals with backbones, called vertebrates, appeared in the Devonian Period. Among them were the first fishes.

Only very primitive animals like sponges and jellyfish existed until 600 million years ago.

Animals without backbones appeared from 570 million to 390 million years ago during the Paleozoic Era.

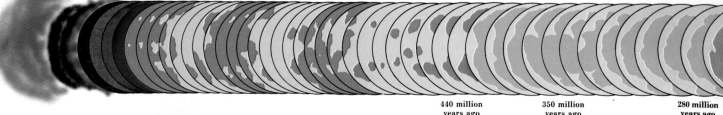

				440 million years ago	350 million years ago	280 million years ago
Precambrian Era	Cambrian Period	Ordovician Period	Silurian Period	Devonian Period	Carboniferous Period	Per
				Paleozoic Era		
4.6 billion years ago	600 million years ago	500 million years ago	400 million years ago	300 million years ago		

6

In the Permian Period more froglike creatures developed, and the first reptiles began to appear.

7

At the start of the Triassic Period there were many reptiles, and the first dinosaurs began to appear.

8

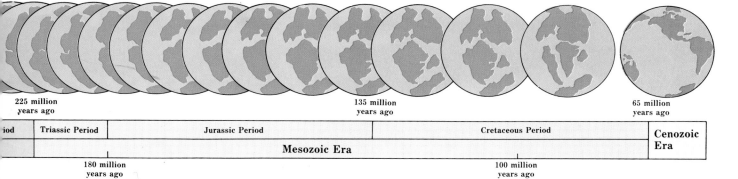

The Jurassic Period was the dinosaurs' golden age, and there were many allosaurs, stegosaurs and apatosaurs.

● **To the Parent**

The earth began to form about 4.6 billion years ago, and single-celled organisms made their appearance about 3.1 billion years ago. Life evolved from these simple forms to the more complex vertebrates including reptiles, which appeared in the late Carboniferous Period. Dinosaurs emerged in the Triassic, flourished and multiplied in the Jurassic and Cretaceous Periods and then became extinct.

10

By the Cenozoic Era mammals and birds dominated the earth, and all the dinosaurs had disappeared.

9

During the Cretaceous Period Tyrannosaurus and Triceratops appeared, as did the first true birds.

| | 225 million years ago | | 135 million years ago | | 65 million years ago |

iod	Triassic Period	Jurassic Period	Cretaceous Period	Cenozoic Era
		Mesozoic Era		
	180 million years ago		100 million years ago	

Where Did Dinosaurs Come From?

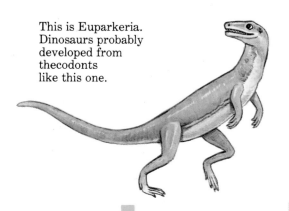

This is Euparkeria. Dinosaurs probably developed from thecodonts like this one.

ANSWER All animals develop from other animals. This process, called evolution, takes a very long time. Scientists believe that dinosaurs evolved from creatures called thecodonts. These animals lived before dinosaurs. They ate meat and small insects.

Scientists study fossil remains of dinosaurs. That is why they think that dinosaurs evolved from thecodonts.

■ How did thecodonts stand and move?

Thecodonts had long, strong back legs. Their front legs were short and weak. They could stand almost straight on their back legs. They could run very fast too.

● **To the Parent**

The dinosaurs' ancestors are thought to have been a group of smallish reptiles called thecodonts. Dinosaurs may have evolved from a creature like Euparkeria about 230 million years ago. Euparkeria's skull, hips and leg bones have features distinct from those of other reptiles. Its bone structure indicates that it could walk either on four feet or nearly erect on its well-developed, straight hind legs. Fossils found in Africa indicate that it stood about two feet (60 cm) high.

▼ Euparkeria (front) and Saltoposuchus (back) are examples of thecodonts.

Were Any of the Dinosaurs Able to Swim or Fly?

ANSWER No. Dinosaurs lived only on land. But other creatures lived during the same time as the dinosaurs. Pterosaurs could fly. Some pterosaurs were as small as sparrows. Others were bigger than any of today's birds. Several kinds of creatures swam in the water.

Dinosaurs could not fly.

Dinosaurs

Dinosaurs could not swim or live under water.

Ichthyosaurs

Ichthyosaurs were sea creatures and could live only in the water.

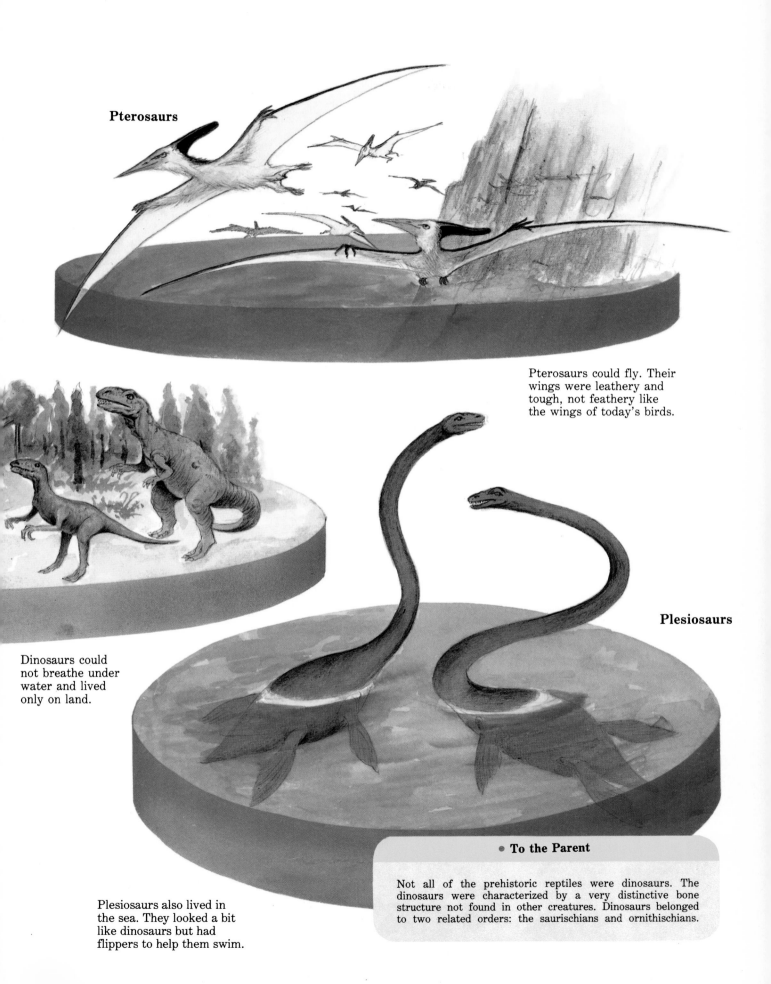

Pterosaurs

Pterosaurs could fly. Their wings were leathery and tough, not feathery like the wings of today's birds.

Plesiosaurs

Dinosaurs could not breathe under water and lived only on land.

Plesiosaurs also lived in the sea. They looked a bit like dinosaurs but had flippers to help them swim.

● **To the Parent**

Not all of the prehistoric reptiles were dinosaurs. The dinosaurs were characterized by a very distinctive bone structure not found in other creatures. Dinosaurs belonged to two related orders: the saurischians and ornithischians.

11

Did All Dinosaurs Live at the Same Time?

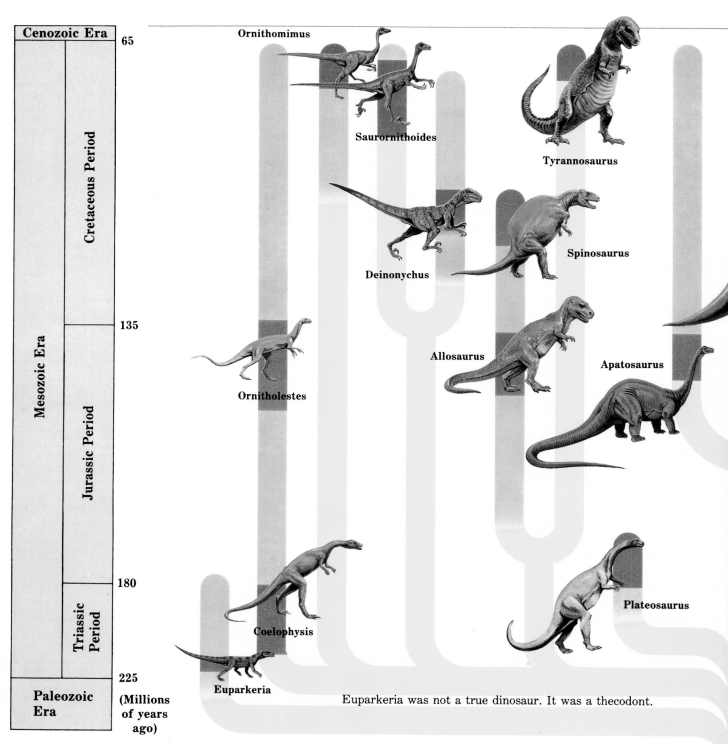

Cenozoic Era		65
Mesozoic Era	**Cretaceous Period**	
		135
	Jurassic Period	
		180
	Triassic Period	
		225
Paleozoic Era		(Millions of years ago)

Ornithomimus

Saurornithoides

Tyrannosaurus

Deinonychus

Spinosaurus

Ornitholestes

Allosaurus

Apatosaurus

Coelophysis

Plateosaurus

Euparkeria

Euparkeria was not a true dinosaur. It was a thecodont.

ANSWER Dinosaurs roamed the earth for millions of years. As time passed some kinds died out, and new ones took their place. Today we know of more than 600 different kinds.

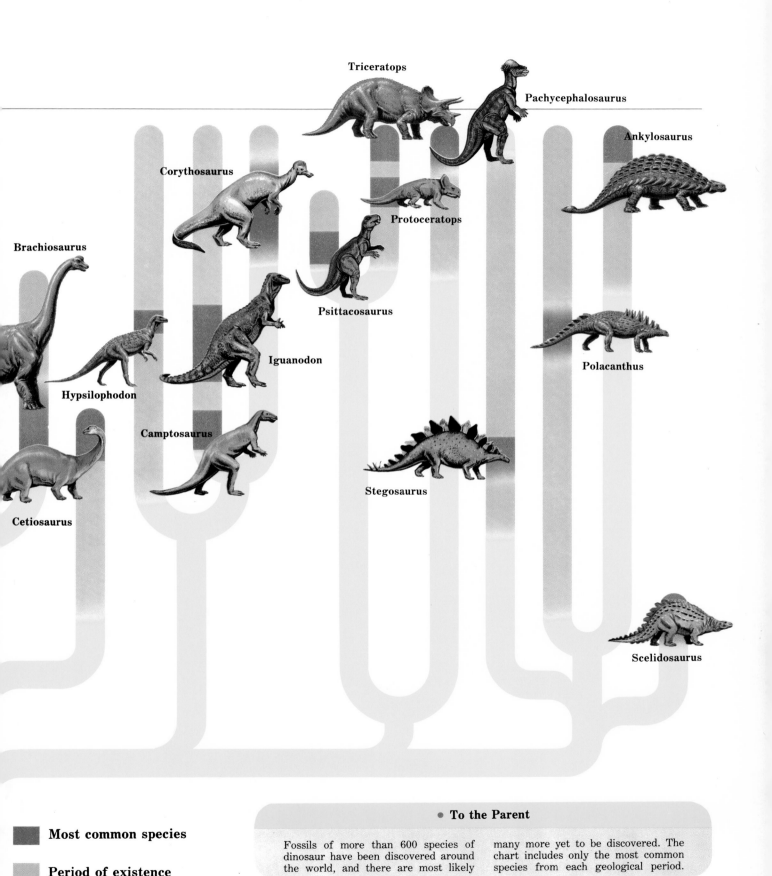

Triceratops

Pachycephalosaurus

Ankylosaurus

Corythosaurus

Protoceratops

Brachiosaurus

Psittacosaurus

Iguanodon

Hypsilophodon

Polacanthus

Camptosaurus

Cetiosaurus

Stegosaurus

Scelidosaurus

Most common species

Period of existence

● **To the Parent**

Fossils of more than 600 species of dinosaur have been discovered around the world, and there are most likely many more yet to be discovered. The chart includes only the most common species from each geological period.

How Did Dinosaurs Get Their Names?

ANSWER Scientists who discover fossils of a dinosaur or other ancient reptile name it. The name may describe the way it looked. Or its name may describe the way it behaved. Some dinosaurs are named after the place where the fossils were discovered.

Tyrannosaurus

This fierce beast's name means tyrant lizard.

Oviraptor

Its name means egg stealer. Scientists think this dinosaur took the eggs of other dinosaurs and ate them.

Deinonychus

Its name means terrible claw. The dinosaur's name refers to the huge claw on its hind legs.

Albertosaurus

This dinosaur is named for the Canadian province of Alberta. That's where its fossils were discovered.

Stegosaurus

It was given the name roofed lizard because the large plates running down its back looked like the tiled roofs of houses.

Iguanodon

This was one of the first dinosaurs ever discovered. Its teeth looked like those of a modern lizard called an iguana.

Pteranodon

This creature had no teeth in its jaw. Its name, which means winged toothless one, makes perfect sense.

Triceratops

The name means three-horned face. Can you see the horns?

Sordes pilosus

This flying reptile was covered with rough hair and looked fierce. That's why scientists gave it a name that means hairy devil.

Ichthyosaurus

This reptile lived in the sea. Instead of legs it had fins and paddles, which helped it glide through the water. Scientists gave it a name that means fish lizard.

● To the Parent

A dinosaur is commonly known by the scientific name given to the first fossil of its kind discovered and cataloged. The animal's scientific name shows its genus and species. In Tyrannosaurus rex, Tyrannosaurus is the genus name and rex is the species name. Both names are written in Latin, and the genus name is capitalized, but the species name is not capitalized. Names in this book are written like that.

What Did Dinosaurs Eat?

ANSWER Dinosaurs ate the kinds of things that animals eat today. They can be divided into two main groups. The meat eaters fed on the flesh of other animals. Such creatures are known as carnivores. The other dinosaurs ate only plants. Animals that eat plants are called herbivores.

Parasaurolophus

This gentle giant live on the leaves, twigs and cones of fir trees.

Compsognathus

A small meat eater about the size of a chicken, it ate smaller animals such as lizards.

Diplodocus

With its long neck it was able to pick the choicest leaves from the tops of the trees.

Saurornithoides

This is another meat eater. It probably ate the first tiny mammals and small lizards.

Deinonychus

This meat eater was one of the fiercest of the smaller dinosaurs.

Baryonyx

The claws on its front paws helped this meat eater catch lots of fish.

● **To the Parent**

There is little fossilized evidence of what dinosaurs ate. Certain exceptions are the Compsognathus, Baryonyx and Hadrosaurus, the contents of whose stomachs have been found fossilized intact. Evidence that Deinonychus preyed on Tenontosaurus also has been discovered. The diet of the majority of dinosaurs can only be guessed at based on data that researchers obtain from the fossilized teeth.

Stegosaurus

It was a heavily armored plant eater and grazed on shrubs and ferns or on tall plants.

Oviraptor

The egg thief raided the nests of other dinosaurs for food.

Tyrannosaurus

This was the most famous meat eater of all. It fed mostly on large, slow-moving dinosaurs that could not escape from it.

17

How Were Meat Eaters Different From Plant Eaters?

ANSWER The biggest difference in these two groups of dinosaurs can be seen by looking closely at their teeth. Meat eaters had long, sharp teeth for cutting and chewing. Plant eaters had many even, flat teeth for grinding up their food.

Lambeosaurus, a herbivore

Plant eaters had teeth designed for plucking and grinding plants.

Chew these very well!

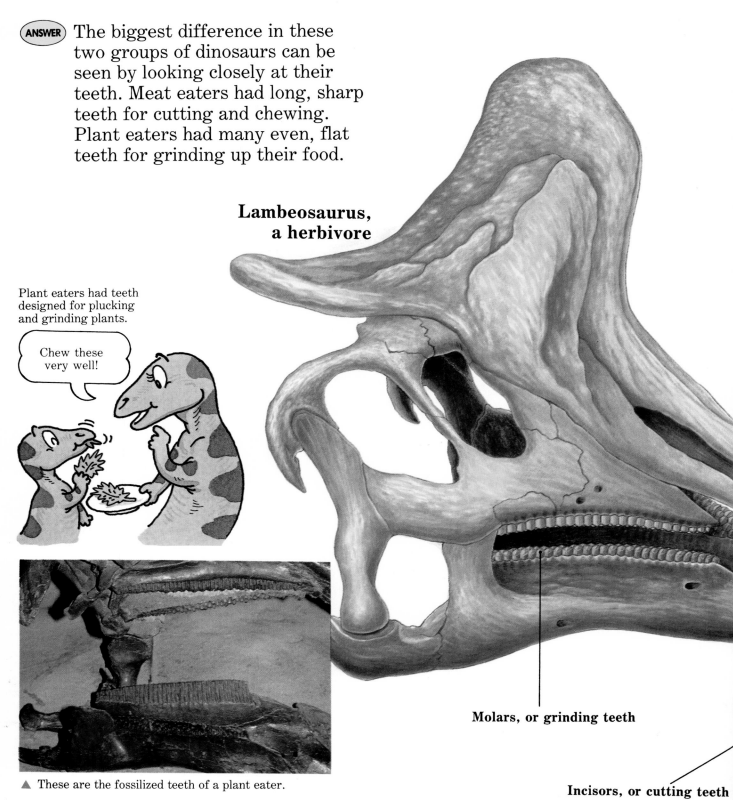

▲ These are the fossilized teeth of a plant eater.

Molars, or grinding teeth

Incisors, or cutting teeth

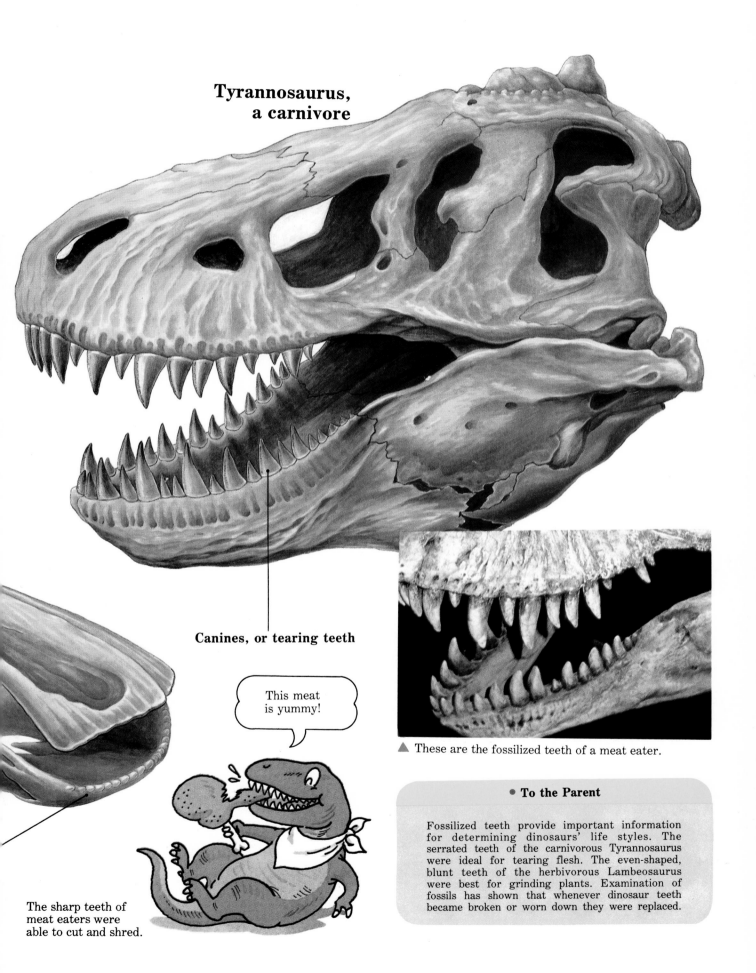

**Tyrannosaurus,
a carnivore**

Canines, or tearing teeth

This meat
is yummy!

▲ These are the fossilized teeth of a meat eater.

The sharp teeth of
meat eaters were
able to cut and shred.

● **To the Parent**

Fossilized teeth provide important information
for determining dinosaurs' life styles. The
serrated teeth of the carnivorous Tyrannosaurus
were ideal for tearing flesh. The even-shaped,
blunt teeth of the herbivorous Lambeosaurus
were best for grinding plants. Examination of
fossils has shown that whenever dinosaur teeth
became broken or worn down they were replaced.

How Did Dinosaurs Fight?

(ANSWER) Meat eaters had sharp teeth and claws for hunting and fighting. Plant eaters were often covered with plates like armor or had a tail with spikes on it. This helped protect them from attackers.

■ How did dinosaurs attack prey?

Allosaurus used its sharp teeth to fight dinosaurs bigger than it was.

Deinonychus had claws that opened quickly whenever it attacked.

Baryonyx had claws on both its front legs.

■ A plant eater's defenses

Triceratops had three long, sharp horns to fight with.

Tyrannosaurus versus Triceratops

Stegosaurus defended itself by using the long, sharp spikes at the end of its tail.

Ankylosaurus had a tail with a large lump of bone at the end which was used like a club.

Pachycephalosaurus butted its enemies with its head.

Iguanodon had huge claws like thumbs to protect itself.

● **To the Parent**

The sharp cutting teeth of the larger carnivores were their most useful weapons. To defend themselves against these predators the smaller plant eaters over millions of years developed a goodly number of assorted weapons and tactics. They grew horns and claws, strong tails or heads, and perfected butting, scratching and clawing techniques.

Were Dinosaurs Smart?

ANSWER At first people did not think they were very smart. Although their bodies were big their brains were believed to be very small. Now people know more about dinosaurs. For animals of their size their brains were about the same as today's reptiles. In some cases dinosaurs had bigger brains and were smarter than today's reptiles. Still, compared to people these creatures were not very smart.

Although dinosaurs were smarter than was once thought, they could never have been able to do many of the things that people can. They did not have enough brainpower.

■ The brain of a Stegosaurus

The Stegosaurus gave dinosaurs their reputation for stupidity. An adult Stegosaurus measured 20 feet (6 m) from nose to tail and weighed more than 1.7 tons (1.5 t). Yet its brain weighed no more than three ounces (85 g). It is still not known why its brain was so tiny. The brains of other dinosaurs were found to be much larger.

■ A dinosaur's nervous system

Just as it was once believed that all dinosaurs were not smart they were also thought to have had simple nervous systems. It was once thought that if a dinosaur was hurt it would take a long time for the pain to get to its brain since its body was so large. But that was not true. Their nervous system brought this pain quickly to their brain so they could feel it.

One story that used to be believed about dinosaurs was that they didn't realize it when someone was stepping on their tail.

Brain

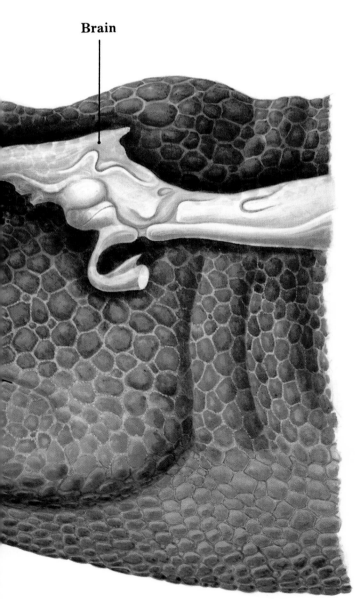

■ Did dinosaurs have good eyes?

Scientists believe that dinosaurs had good eyesight. They could probably tell one color from another one.

■ Could they hear and smell well?

These senses were also well developed. Dinosaurs probably had sharp hearing and a good sense of smell.

● **To the Parent**

Seeking to unravel the mysteries surrounding the dinosaurs, early paleontologists asserted that dinosaurs were ungainly and slow-witted too. While larger animals seem to have greater difficulty overcoming inertia, and also tend to move slowly, this is a result of dynamics and is not related to intelligence. It is now believed that some dinosaurs were smart and were able to perform fairly difficult activities. Some of them might even have demonstrated social behavior.

? Were Dinosaurs Cold-blooded Like Today's Reptiles?

ANSWER Cold-blooded animals cannot control the temperature of their bodies. They move around when the weather is warm and must rest when it is cold. Today's reptiles are all cold-blooded creatures. Scientists used to think all dinosaurs were like this too. Now they think that some were warm-blooded, like birds and mammals. One warm-blooded dinosaur was Deinonychus.

▲ The crocodile we see today is cold-blooded.

Deinonychus attacking Tenontosaurus

■ Warm-blooded dinosaurs: a new way of thinking

A warm body temperature gives us the energy to move around. In cold weather the body temperature of cold-blooded animals drops and they become inactive. Because reptiles are cold-blooded they avoid moving around much at night and hibernate in winter. Birds and mammals are warm-blooded so their bodies remain warm even in cold weather. They can be active day and night in both summer and winter. Because dinosaurs also seem to have been active nights and winters it is possible that some were warm-blooded.

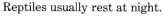

Reptiles usually rest at night.   Reptiles sleep through winter.

If dinosaurs were warm-blooded, they would have been able to control their body heat.

Some dinosaurs might have been warm-blooded. Like birds and mammals they were not greatly affected by hot or cold weather.

■ Cold-blooded and active: another possible answer

Fossils suggest that dinosaurs were active, warm-blooded animals. But it is still possible that they were not. The earth's climate was much warmer, and the winters were not as cold when some dinosaurs lived. Because the dinosaurs were so huge they would lose body heat more slowly. So perhaps they were both cold-blooded and active.

It appears that dinosaurs may have been active all year.

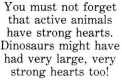
You must not forget that active animals have strong hearts. Dinosaurs might have had very large, very strong hearts too!

● **To the Parent**

Recently there have been arguments as to whether the dinosaurs were warm-blooded or cold-blooded. It is very hard to determine for sure though evidence shows that they were probably active, fast-moving animals. Since they were active even in cooler temperatures they must have been able to control their body temperature without regard to whether they were cold-blooded or warm-blooded.

❓ Which Dinosaur Was Largest?

ANSWER Ultrasaurus must have been the biggest dinosaur of all. None has been found that was larger. One Ultrasaurus found in Colorado in 1979 was more than 100 feet (30 m) long, stood 60 feet (18 m) tall and weighed 152 tons (137 t). The name Ultrasaurus means largest lizard. This monster dinosaur may have been a relative of Brachiosaurus.

■ How did Ultrasaurus get that name?

It got that name because it was enormous. It was as tall as a five-story building and weighed almost as much as a 747 jumbo jet.

● **To the Parent**

Before Ultrasaurus was found, the largest dinosaur known had been Brachiosaurus, which was 50 feet (15 m) long and 40 feet tall, and sometimes weighed as much as 85 tons (76 t). But the discovery of the fossil in Colorado showed a creature so huge that it was immediately dubbed Ultrasaurus since it seemed to be the ultimate in size. Its actual scientific name is yet to be decided upon, so it continues to be known as the ultimate one. Research is now aimed at establishing a relationship between this giant and its massive relative, the herbivorous Brachiosaurus.

Ultrasaurus was a plant eater and might have lived in herds much the way elephants do today.

Why Was Brachiosaurus So Big?

(ANSWER) Brachiosaurus lived at a time when the earth's climate was warm and wet. The planet was covered with tall trees. Brachiosaurus was a plant eater. It fed on leaves near the tops of trees. It could not stand on its back legs to reach these leaves. Instead Brachiosaurus grew very tall with a long, strong neck.

Brachiosaurus was more than 50 feet (15 m) long and often weighed more than 85 tons (77 t). It had plenty to eat and didn't have to hunt for food. Like today's largest animals it grew large because it needed little energy to live.

Of all the animals on earth today the largest ones are those that don't have to use much energy finding food.

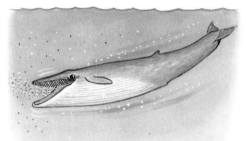

Blue whales eat a lot but don't use much energy staying alive either. And they are the largest animals that ever lived.

■ Why do things get bigger?

Animals have a pituitary gland which acts like a control box. It tells the body when and how much to grow. It stops mammals when they've grown enough but lets reptiles grow as big as they can. The pituitary gland of some dinosaurs let them grow to huge sizes.

Pituitary gland

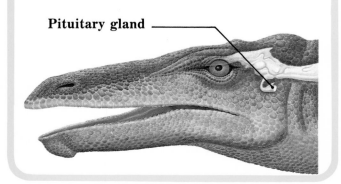

■ Didn't dinosaurs ever stop growing?

Mammals stop growing once they have become adults, but reptiles go on growing until the day they die!

• **To the Parent**

During the Jurassic Period the earth's climate was warm with very little seasonal variation. Plant life was abundant, providing herbivores in particular with a constant and plentiful food supply all year round. In this environment Brachiosaurus and its relatives were able to eat huge amounts while expending little energy. Consequently they grew enormously. Great expenditures of energy limit the potential size of living things.

What's So Big About Being Big?

■ Bigger stays warm longer

Reptiles are cold-blooded. Their body heat rises and falls with the climate. If they have small bodies, they lose or gain body heat quickly. With their bigger bodies dinosaurs that were cold-blooded would lose their body heat more slowly and stay active longer. This was one good thing about being so large.

When it gets cold, small lizards become sleepy and inactive. They hardly move at all, even to catch food, until the temperature rises.

Because it was so huge and lost body heat slowly the enormous Brachiosaurus remained active even when temperatures dropped.

■ Bigger is safer

Simply being big is a good defense against small animals. A smaller dinosaur, even if it is very fierce, might not attack one that was much bigger. It would be frightened of one larger than itself. The size of a brachiosaur was a good defense against enemies like allosaurs and other fierce, meat-eating dinosaurs.

A lion won't attack an elephant because the elephant is so big that it could crush the lion.

For the same reason smaller, fiercer meat eaters probably did not attack the big brachiosaurs.

■ Tall can reach higher

The taller a dinosaur the higher it could reach for food. Dinosaurs that couldn't reach the tall trees would have to go looking for their food. Brachiosaurus stood much higher than other dinosaurs and had a very long neck. It ate from the trees that shorter dinosaurs could not reach.

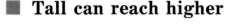

With its height a giraffe can reach the treetops to graze. The smaller gazelle cannot.

Brachiosaurus grazed like giraffes but from treetops that were twice as high.

Why Did Apatosaurus Have Such an Enormous Tail?

ANSWER The Apatosaurus had a thick heavy body and four sturdy legs. It weighed as much as 34 tons (31 t). It needed a very long tail to balance the weight of its head, neck and body. Without this tail it would not have been able to walk.

▲ The skull was missing from this almost perfect Apatosaurus skeleton, but it must have looked something like this.

Without a tail to balance it Apatosaurus couldn't have kept its head off the ground.

Apatosaurus was one of many kinds of brontosaurs. It was misnamed Brontosaurus or thunder lizard at first by scientists who thought it looked like a lizard and was so huge that it must have made a sound like thunder with every step that it took.

■ Facts from fossils

Everything known about Apatosaurus comes from fossils. Their skeletons show that they were plant eaters and large enough to eat from the tops of tall trees. One footprint the size of a child's wading pool shows how enormous their feet were.

It is also believed that Apatosaurus traveled in herds like elephants do today, with the young in the center and the adults on the outside for protection. They did not drag those giant tails when they walked but lifted them off the ground.

● To the Parent

The blue whale is the largest animal on earth today. In fact it is probably the largest that has ever lived. Supported by salty ocean water an adult blue whale can grow to weigh a stupendous 190 tons (170 t). On land Apatosaurus at 34 tons (30 t) and Ultrasaurus at 152 tons (136 t) could function as exclusively terrestrial animals, supporting their great weights on their huge legs alone. Brontosaurs not only survived, they flourished by evolving a skeletal structure capable of supporting their enormous bodies. Dynamics of balance, not unlike those applied to a suspension bridge, supported the heavy body between a long neck and tail. Even so their bulk kept brontosaurs firmly among the plodders and well out of the ranks of the small, more active herbivores and the highly active predatory carnivores of the time. But they all died at the same time.

There were more than 80 bones in that tail. Just carrying it was a big job.

31

Were All Dinosaurs So Big?

 ANSWER It is a mistake to think that all dinosaurs were big. Look at Compsognathus. This dinosaur was two feet (60 cm) long. Other dinosaurs were probably smaller than this one.

Compsognathus

Were some of them small?

Many dinosaurs were no larger than today's house cat. Some that lived in the Triassic or in the beginning of the Jurassic Period were even smaller.

Cat

Compare some of these smaller dinosaurs with the size of a domestic cat.

Saltopus was only two feet (60 cm) long.

Echinodon was also two feet (60 cm) long.

Lesothosaurus was three feet (91 cm) long.

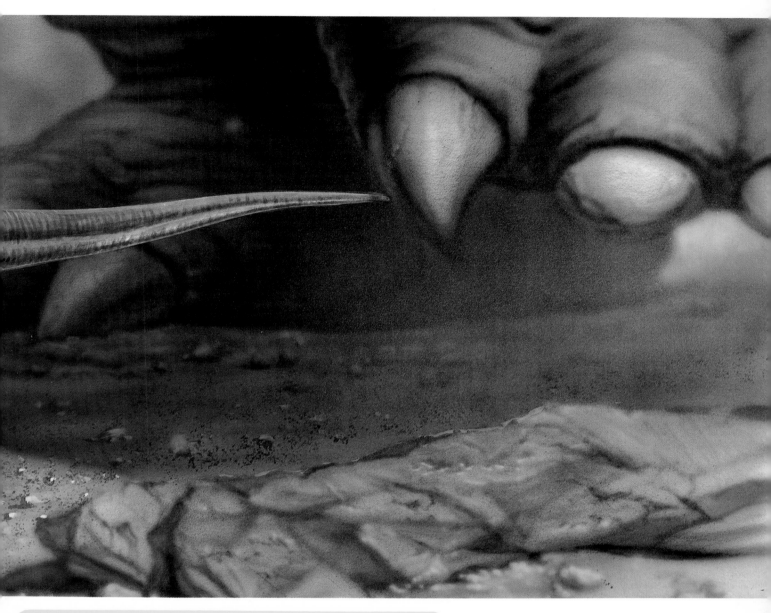

Small, swift and agile

The smallest dinosaurs needed to move quickly if they were to survive. That would make it hard for bigger, slow-moving meat eaters to catch them.

Oh my! I must get out of here!

● **To the Parent**

Coelurosaurs and fabrosaurids, two groups that appeared in the Triassic and lived during the Jurassic, were mainly smaller dinosaurs. They were tiny compared to the giants that evolved at the end of the Jurassic and on into the Cretaceous Period.

? Which Dinosaur Was Strongest?

ANSWER Tyrannosaurus rex was the strongest dinosaur of all. Its name means king of the tyrant lizards. A full-grown Tyrannosaurus measured 46 feet (14 m) from head to tail, making it the largest meat eater to ever walk the earth. It had sharp teeth and a very powerful jaw for fighting other large dinosaurs. It was a scavenger. That means it ate dead animals.

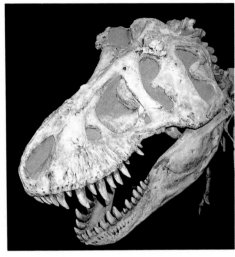

▲ This skull was Tyrannosaurus rex.

Tyrannosaurus attacking a Corythosaurus

Other Smaller But Fierce Dinosaurs

Deinonychus and Dromaeosaurus were small but vicious hunters. Deinonychus, or terrible claw, had big, sharp claws on its back feet to slash its prey. Dromaeosaurus had sharp claws too.

Deinonychus would seize, then rip, kick and tear its victim to pieces.

■ Dromaeosaurus' movable claws

It ran with its claws pulled in.

It kept its balance by extending its tail.

■ Unsheathing its terrible claws

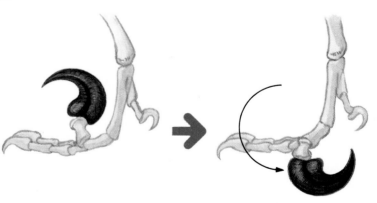

Its claws were movable. When it needed to fight for food or to protect itself the claws came out so the dromaeosaur could use them as weapons.

● **To the Parent**

While Tyrannosaurus was the largest carnivore and strongest predator that ever lived, scientists are unsure how aggressive it could have been, given its bulk. The most aggressive predators are usually the compact, fast and agile animals. But there is no way to judge how agile these huge, extinct animals were.

Why Did Tyrannosaurus Have Such Small Front Legs?

ANSWER Tyrannosaurus walked on its strong back legs. It used its powerful teeth and jaws to fight other dinosaurs. Since Tyrannosaurus made little use of its front legs, or forelegs, they finally became much smaller and weaker.

While scavenging, a tyrannosaur comes upon the carcass of a Hadrosaurus.

▲ Albertosaurus had underdeveloped forelegs like its cousin Tyrannosaurus.

Were a Tyrannosaur's Front Legs Useless?

Even the small forelegs were of some use. Tyrannosaurus used its front legs for holding food. It probably also used them to help it up off the ground after resting.

It lies on its belly.

It raises its body.

It stands on its legs.

● **To the Parent**

There are many unanswered questions about tyrannosaurs, like the usefulness of their underdeveloped forelegs. Allosaurus, the largest Jurassic carnivore, had mighty, three-toed forelegs, which it used in hunting its prey. By comparison a tyrannosaur's tiny, two-toed forelegs must have been useless for hunting, which suggests the possibility that it was more a scavenger than a killer.

Which Dinosaur Could Run Fastest?

ANSWER No one knows for sure. Some people think that Ornithomimus was the fastest. This dinosaur looked like an ostrich without feathers. It had powerful legs and could run very fast like the ostrich. Scientists believe that it could run 50 miles (80 km) per hour.

Ornithomimus had no teeth. That was one of the most special things about it. It is not clear what it ate, but it might have been omnivorous. That is, it ate plants and meat too. It is probable that this dinosaur lived on fruits, seeds, small animals and insects. It may even have eaten the eggs of other dinosaurs.

Who'd win if dinosaurs had a race?

Scientists arrived at these speeds by studying bone and muscle structure, and size and weight.

Apatosaurus
2.5 mph (4 km/h)

Triceratops
31 mph (50 km/h)

Compsognathus
37 mph (60 km/h)

Ornithomimus
50 mph (80 km/h)

• **To the Parent**

How fast an animal can run is closely related to the placement and height of its hips. It is possible to estimate the speeds of extinct species based on the skeleton and musculature and a comparison with living animals. Ornithomimus could reach 50 miles per hour (80 km/h), a bit slower than an ostrich. An obscure animal named Dromiceiomimus may have been even faster.

How Did Stegosaurus Use the Plates on Its Back?

(ANSWER) Those bony plates may have helped protect Stegosaurus from attack. Scientists believe that the dinosaur also used them to control its body temperature. You can see in the drawings below how its temperature might have been regulated.

■ To protect itself

Perhaps plates were a defense against attacking meat eaters.

■ To adjust its body heat

In cooler weather Stegosaurus might have lifted the plates to catch the sun's warmth.

When it was warm enough it could lower its plates.

Stegosaurus might even have raised and lowered its plates to catch a cool breeze and lower its body temperature that way.

● **To the Parent**

It is generally assumed that Stegosaurus' bony back plates served a dual purpose: as a defense mechanism against predatory carnivores and as a kind of thermostat for raising or lowering body temperature by absorbing or deflecting solar energy. Surface heat exchangers and a maze of blood vessels could have completed this effort.

❓ Why Did Kentrosaurus Have Such Sharp Spikes?

ANSWER Kentrosaurus' name means prickly lizard. It is easy to see why it was called that. The dinosaur had sharp spikes running from the middle of its back down its tail. It used them when it fought.

■ Kentrosaurus using its spikes

When attacked by an enemy Kentrosaurus could swing its heavy tail and stab with its spikes.

It had spikes on the back and tail.

The double tail spike was a deadly weapon.

It might have looked clumsy, but Kentrosaurus was very agile. It could wheel around and deliver a fatal blow with its back or tail spikes before an attacker could flip it over to get at its unprotected belly.

Kentrosaurus grazing

● **To the Parent**

Kentrosaurus lived in the late Jurassic Period in what is now Tanzania. It was the most elaborately armored stegosaur. Although it looked ungainly it had a superb pivot mechanism in the hips which allowed it to swivel around easily. Designed to eat things in high places, it rose easily on its hind legs with support from its tail. Plates and spikes deterred a predator from biting it and could ward off an attack from any direction. One swing from its formidable tail could have been lethal.

What Big Dinosaur Was the Armored Tank of Its Time?

ANSWER The dinosaur was named Ankylosaurus. It was covered from head to tail with thick, bony plates. It also had spikes on the sides of its body. At the end of its tail was a thick, heavy bone, which it could swing at its enemies. This dinosaur was a plant eater. It used its plates, spikes and tail only to protect itself from attackers.

Ankylosaurus fights off Tyrannosaurus with a tremendous blow from its tail.

44

How Ankylosaurus defended itself

Ankylosaurus had bony plates two inches (5 cm) thick right down its back and tail. The heavy, bony club at the end of its tail was an excellent weapon.

Even with its razor-sharp teeth a meat eater would not have been able to bite through such armor plating. It was too thick and bony for that.

▲ This museum model shows what Ankylosaurus' armor looked like.

Ankylosaurus defended itself by swinging its bony war club. One blow could break the bones of a meat eater.

Ankylosaurus had no armor on its underside. Its weak point was its soft, unprotected belly. If enemies managed to flip it over onto its back they could kill it.

Different species of ankylosaurs

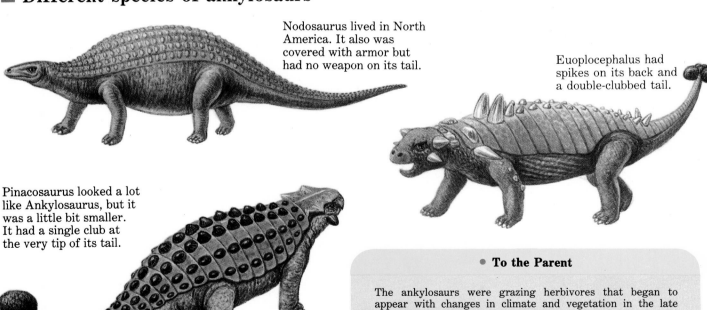

Nodosaurus lived in North America. It also was covered with armor but had no weapon on its tail.

Euoplocephalus had spikes on its back and a double-clubbed tail.

Pinacosaurus looked a lot like Ankylosaurus, but it was a little bit smaller. It had a single club at the very tip of its tail.

• To the Parent

The ankylosaurs were grazing herbivores that began to appear with changes in climate and vegetation in the late Jurassic. They were almost the last to die out during the great dying that closed the Cretaceous. Most of them had bony armor and tails that ended in the form of a club. The longest of this suborder was Ankylosaurus at 26 feet (8 m).

Which Dinosaur Could Have Been Called Old Bonehead?

ANSWER The prize for the thickest skull goes to Pachycephalosaurus. Its name means thick-headed lizard. The top of its skull was nearly 10 inches (25 cm) thick. It protected itself by butting other dinosaurs with its head.

Like today's rams, these creatures would butt heads to win over females of the herd.

■ What its skull looked like

Old bonehead's unique feature was that thick skull. These beasts seem to have done a lot of fighting, and that was their main weapon.

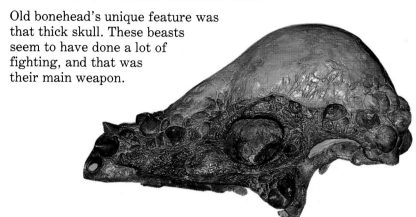

● **To the Parent**

Pachycephalosaurs were herbivores that fed on lowland grasses. They appeared in the early Cretaceous Period. Their thick skulls gave them an erudite appearance in addition to the name of dome heads, but these skulls protected an unexceptional brain. Nevertheless that massive bone grew on these creatures for some reason. It may be that dome heads used their heads as a weapon of defense and attack. It is likely they engaged in head-butting contests to determine the leader of the herd or the consort of a harem of females, similar to the methods of the bighorn sheep of today.

▼ Dinosaurs butt heads in a contest for leadership.

Which Group of Dinosaurs Had Horns?

ANSWER One group of dinosaurs was named the ceratopsids. That word means horned face. The best known of the horned dinosaurs was named Triceratops, or three-horned face. Triceratops looked very much like today's rhinoceros.

▲ The spiny Styracosaurus had a horned snout and neck frills ending in long spikes.

▲ Triceratops, the most famous ceratopsid, had three horns. It was 30 feet (9 m) long from nose to tail.

▲ Pentaceratops had a high, curved neck frill, with very long horns on its head and snout.

▲ Like other horned dinosaurs Centrosaurus had a covering on its neck called a frill. There were two horns near the top of its neck frill and a horn on its snout.

Pentaceratops was wrongly named. Instead of five horns, it had three horns plus two pointed cheekbones.

Triceratopses face down a Tyrannosaurus. ▶

● **To the Parent**

Ceratopsids were large-horned herbivores that thrived at the end of the Cretaceous Period. In addition to a horn on the snout, most of them also sported multiple horns on the head and cheek and on the edges of elaborate neck frills. With such weaponry they were probably quite proficient in facing down a predatory carnivore. Their curved, beak-like snouts were another distinguishing feature. Resemblance to the rhinoceros of today is strong, though it seems to be only a superficial coincidence.

How Many Eggs Did a Dinosaur Lay?

ANSWER Very few nests with dinosaur eggs have been found. It is known that a duckbilled dinosaur named Hadrosaurus laid up to 30 eggs. Protoceratops, a horned dinosaur, laid 30 to 35 eggs. What a big family that would have made.

A Hadrosaurus lays its eggs.

▲ A baby Hadrosaurus skeleton was found beside a nest in which several eggs were laid.

▲ A female Protoceratops stands guard by its nest.

■ Finding Protoceratops eggs

Many fossils of Protoceratops together with its nest, or clutch, of eggs and its young have been found in Central Asia's Gobi Desert. Scientists could identify the fossils as Protoceratops because some eggs were close to being hatched. Adults were found near the nest, showing that they stayed at the nest until the young hatched.

▲ This fossil shows a Protoceratops hatching.

Protoceratops had no horns, but it was a true ceratopsid. It was the ancestor of the most famous of all ceratopsids, Triceratops, the three-horned giant.

● **To the Parent**

Finds of Hadrosaurus and Protoceratops with their nests and their eggs are the only existing fossil data that point to dinosaur methods of egg laying. Yet scientists are sure that other dinosaurs also laid eggs and that they protected the clutch during incubation and hatching.

❓ Did Dinosaurs Care for Their Young?

(ANSWER) There was at least one dinosaur that cared for its young. It was a member of the Hadrosauridae family of duckbilled dinosaurs. It was found with fossils of its eggs and one of its babies. That probably means that it cared for its young. And that is the reason that this dinosaur was named Maiasaura, or good-mother lizard. Chances are that certain other dinosaurs cared for their babies too.

How Maiasaura made its nest

First it made an earth mound with a hollow for the eggs.

Then it laid from two to 30 eggs in the hollow it had made.

It covered the eggs with earth to protect them from thieves.

● **To the Parent**

A surprising discovery in Montana in 1978 included a group of nests in mound shapes containing the fossilized remains of a young dinosaur measuring three feet (91 cm) in length, with pieces of eggshell. The teeth of the infant were worn, indicating that it had been fed, maybe by its parents. This previously unknown species of Hadrosaurus was given the name Maiasaura, meaning good-mother lizard, as a result. Fully grown Maiasaura measured about 30 feet (9 m) from head to toe.

Why Did Some Dinosaurs Have a Crest on Their Head?

ANSWER Hadrosaur is the name for the different kinds of duckbilled dinosaurs. Some had crests or crowns on their heads. One of these was Lambeosaurus. The young ones had a small crest that grew larger. The crest may have been a way to tell males from females.

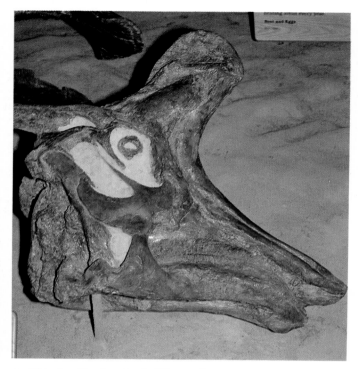

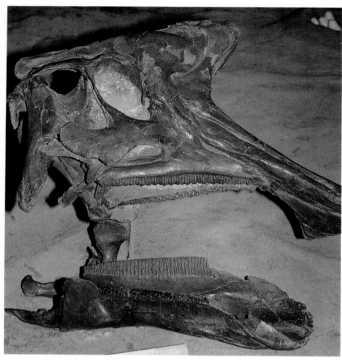

▲ This fossilized male skull has a fancy crest.

▲ The female Lambeosaurus had a simpler crest.

ANSWER ② The answer to this question may have to do with the shape of a dinosaur's crest. Although many hadrosaurs had crests, each group had its own kind. That helped to tell different groups of hadrosaurs apart.

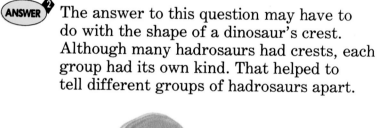

Hypacrosaurus

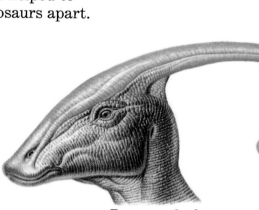

Parasaurolophus

Tsintaosaurus

Corythosaurus

• To the Parent

Hadrosaurs, or duckbilled dinosaurs, are named for their facial features rather than their eating habits. Arriving late on the prehistoric scene, hadrosaurs thrived during the mid-Cretaceous Period. They were distinguished by a variety of head crests, which differed between species and between males and females of the same species. Growth of the crests throughout a duckbill's life suggests that their most likely function was as a secondary sex trait.

? Could Dinosaurs Talk to One Another?

(ANSWER) No one really knows if dinosaurs had voices. Maybe some did and others didn't. Some hadrosaurs had a hollow in their head crest. They may have trumpeted sounds through it almost the way an elephant uses its trunk.

Parasaurolophus and some other hadrosaurs may have been able to trumpet to one another.

▼ Parasaurolophuses trumpet to one another.

■ Skull of Parasaurolophus

The center of the crest was hollow. Perhaps they made a noise in the throat that echoed through the crest. It probably sounded like a loud, clear trumpeting call.

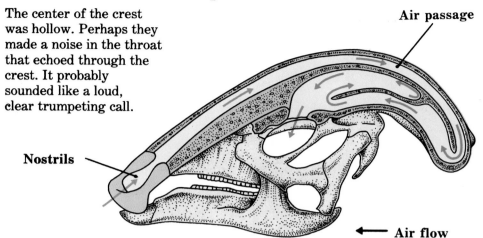

Air passage

Nostrils

← Air flow

● **To the Parent**

Sound leaves no visible record and so the question of whether dinosaurs could communicate may be the most difficult question of all. However, there is fossil evidence to show that the nostrils of Hadrosaurus were elongated. The hollow in the head crest might have acted as a kind of echo chamber: A noise formed in the throat trumpeted through the crest for identification of species, communication, mating and warnings. Parasaurolophus, or the archetypal Hadrosaurus, was named the trombone duckbill because of its facial structure.

❓ Why Did Elasmosaurus Have Such a Long Neck?

ANSWER Elasmosaurus was a reptile that lived in the sea. It is famous for its very long neck. Its neck was twice as long as its body. This reptile used its neck to hunt for food. It reached out and captured sea creatures. Sometimes it reached out of the water to catch flying reptiles called pterosaurs.

Elasmosaurus

Elasmosaurus was able to stretch its long neck high into the air to catch low-flying reptiles or down into the water to catch sea creatures.

The kinds of food Elasmosaurus ate and the unusual way it digested them

Pterosaurus

Fish

Shellfish

Gizzard stones

Elasmosaurus quite likely ate more sea creatures than anything else, with an occasional careless pterosaur snapped out of the air for variety. The sea provided it with fish, shellfish and maybe smaller reptiles.

Elasmosaurus swallowed its food whole much like snakes do today. It also swallowed rocks! The rocks helped digest food in its gizzard. It coughed up the stones when they were worn smooth and then swallowed new one

It preyed on the creatures of the air and the sea, but fossils show that Elasmosaurus was itself preyed on by sharks, which have lived almost unchanged for many millions of years.

Elasmosaurus had about 60 bones in its neck, many more than the giraffe, which has the longest neck today. It has only seven bones.

● To the Parent

Some of the many kinds of plesiosaurs, or early marine reptiles, were long necked. Elasmosaurus, typical of those that were, lived at the end of the Cretaceous. Elasmosaurs may have hunted by plunging their head into a school of fish or snapping up flying pterosaurs. Some elasmosaur fossils found in Kansas show that they had been attacked by sharks quite similar to modern sharks.

? How Did Plesiosaurs Manage to Swim?

ANSWER Plesiosaurs were reptiles that lived in the sea. Some had very long necks, while others did not. These creatures had flippers. They used them much the way today's sea turtles do to glide through the water.

■ How they used their flippers

You might think a plesiosaur's flippers worked the same way that oars in a rowboat do. In fact these sea creatures flapped their flippers. They moved them much the way a bird moves its wings when flying. That is also the way penguins and sea turtles swim.

> ● **To the Parent**
>
> Plesiosaurs had well-developed flippers. Although scientists once thought they used their flippers like oars to move through the water, recent research has led to the theory that plesiosaurs moved them in a shearing or flapping action similar to the way today's sea turtles and penguins propel themselves through the water. However, plesiosaurs could not swim at great speeds with their head out of the water.

Plesiosaurus

How Did Ichthyosaurs Give Birth to Their Young?

ANSWER Most of today's reptiles and fish lay eggs. However, the fish lizards of ancient times were different. Some of them laid eggs, but fossils show that one kind gave birth to live babies.

▲ This fossil shows the actual moment of birth (arrow).

An ichthyosaur gives birth in the ocean.

▲ Known as fast-swimming fish lizards, ichthyosaurs may have leaped over the surface like dolphins.

■ Streamlined for speed

Ichthyosaurus was well suited for life in the sea. Its slim body glided through the water much like the dolphins and swordfish of today.

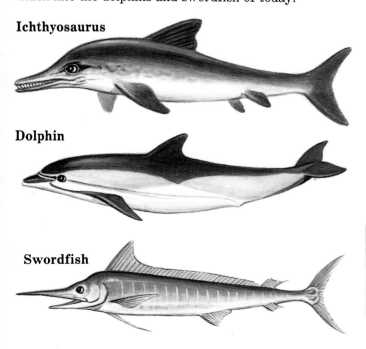

Ichthyosaurus

Dolphin

Swordfish

■ What ichthyosaurs ate

Fish   Shellfish   Shellfish

Ichthyosaurs had rows of sharp teeth to catch food.

● To the Parent

The fossil of Stenopterygius, an ichthyosaur, at the moment of giving birth to its young must constitute one of the most amazing scientific finds ever. It shows that this species at least did not lay eggs. It is possible that other ichthyosaurs were born alive because their fishlike bodies were not equipped to allow them to return to land to lay eggs.

How Did Mosasaurs Eat Hard Shellfish?

ANSWER Mosasaurs were a group of sea reptiles. They were meat eaters that ate whatever they could catch. They had very powerful jaws and sharp teeth for crunching shellfish.

Mosasaurs caught these shellfish with their mouth.

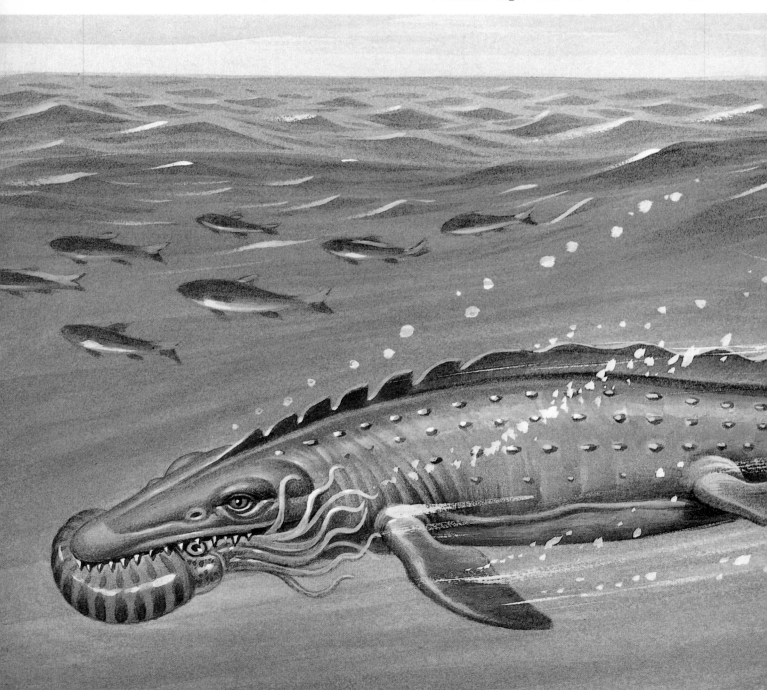

■ A ferocious sea reptile

Mosasaurus was 30 feet (9 m) in length and lived on fish and shellfish. It also ate pterosaurs, which it snatched from the air by leaping out of the sea.

● **To the Parent**

Mosasaurs were sea crocodiles that flourished during the Cretaceous Period. Teleosaurs, maybe the most ferocious of them, appeared at the end of the period. When fully grown, Teleosaurus measured 30 feet (9 m) in length. Mosasaurs probably lived on fish for the most part, although their diet may also have included shellfish and pterosaurs. There is real evidence to support the theory that they also fed on shellfish, because shellfish fossils bearing mosasaur teeth marks have been uncovered. Mosasaurs certainly would have had the power and speed to snap up and devour an unwary pterosaur.

▼ Two fierce mosasaurs catch fish and shellfish.

How Were Pterosaurs Able to Fly?

ANSWER Pterosaurs were flying reptiles. Their wings were made of stiff flaps of skin. They looked a lot like the wings of a bat. Pterosaurs didn't fly as well as birds do today. Pterodactyls are the most famous of the pterosaurs. Pteranodon was a pterodactyl with a huge head crest.

How Pteranodons Got Into the Air

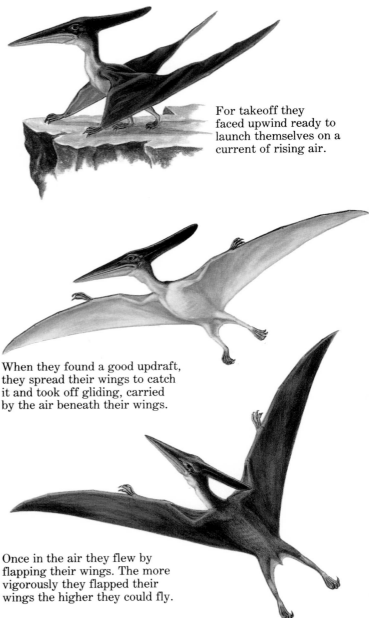

For takeoff they faced upwind ready to launch themselves on a current of rising air.

When they found a good updraft, they spread their wings to catch it and took off gliding, carried by the air beneath their wings.

Once in the air they flew by flapping their wings. The more vigorously they flapped their wings the higher they could fly.

● **To the Parent**

Paleontologists once believed that the wings of pterosaurs were too flimsy to permit true birdlike flight. But fossils discovered in the 1970s showed intact wing membranes with long, stiff connective tissue extending across the reptile's wing. That discovery showed that pterosaurs, an order of flying reptiles that included the genus Pteranodon, in fact could glide and flap and were indeed capable of finely tuned flight. Flight was their survival mechanism, and it kept them flourishing all the way through the Mesozoic Era.

Why Did This Reptile Have Such a Long Tail?

ANSWER This is Rhamphorhynchus. Except for that long tail it looked like other flying reptiles. Scientists think its tail helped this reptile keep its balance while it was gliding or changing direction in the air.

▲ This is how Rhamphorhynchus' skeleton looked.

Some special features of a pterosaur's body

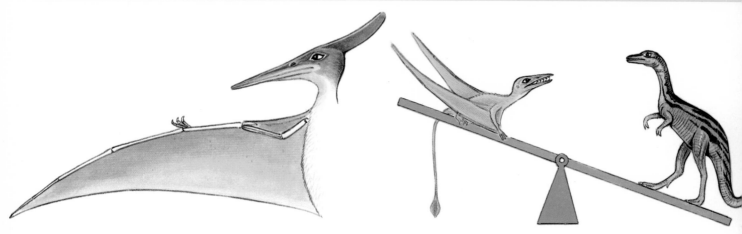

Their wings were formed of strong, fibrous membranes stretching between their bodies and their limbs.

They were good fliers and superb gliders because they were extremely lightweight and had a huge wingspan.

Rhamphorhynchus in flight

They had no feathers but were covered with fur for warmth like some bats today. Moreover, pterosaurs were warm-blooded.

● **To the Parent**

Pterosaurs were divided into two distinct subgroups: long tails and short tails, which were typified by Rhamphorhynchus and Pterodactylus respectively. Pteranodon, a crested short tail, was one of the most advanced. The precise aerodynamic function of Rhamphorhynchus' long tail is not understood, but it is believed to have been instrumental to flight. The blunt and flattened end formed of tough skin over fine, flexible bones must have acted as a rudder for balance and direction control, especially at slow speeds. A self-propelled fish spear with forward-pointing, razor-sharp teeth, it was warm-blooded like all the pterosaurs, as was indicated by fossils found in central Africa.

Was Archaeopteryx Really Descended From Dinosaurs?

ANSWER When the fossil of Archaeopteryx was discovered there was great excitement. This creature was covered with feathers like a bird. It also had teeth, fingers and a tail like a dinosaur. Was this fossil proof that birds descended from dinosaurs? Today scientists think that birds developed separately but at the same time as dinosaurs. They are still not sure how Archaeopteryx developed.

▲ This is a fossilized Archaeopteryx skeleton.

■ Comparison of dinosaurs, Archaeopteryx and birds

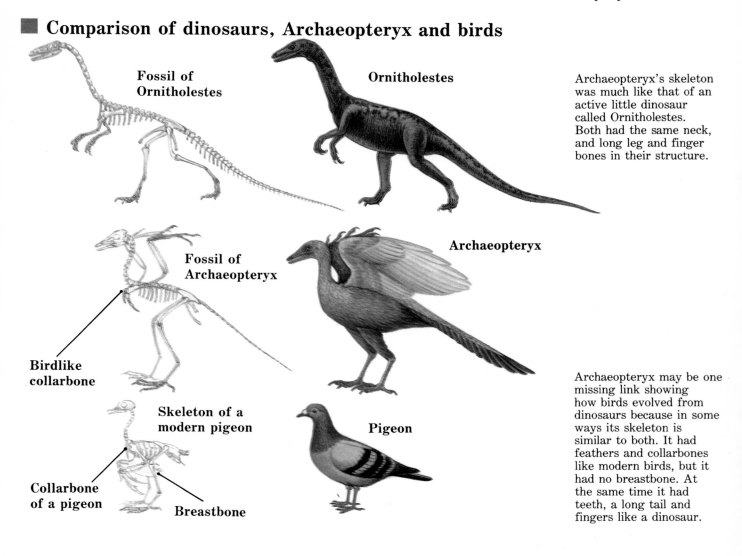

Fossil of Ornitholestes

Ornitholestes

Archaeopteryx's skeleton was much like that of an active little dinosaur called Ornitholestes. Both had the same neck, and long leg and finger bones in their structure.

Fossil of Archaeopteryx

Archaeopteryx

Birdlike collarbone

Skeleton of a modern pigeon

Pigeon

Collarbone of a pigeon

Breastbone

Archaeopteryx may be one missing link showing how birds evolved from dinosaurs because in some ways its skeleton is similar to both. It had feathers and collarbones like modern birds, but it had no breastbone. At the same time it had teeth, a long tail and fingers like a dinosaur.

Archaeopteryx was probably not skilled at flying and could do no more than glide from the trees down to the ground.

■ The oldest creature with true birdlike features

People thought birds were descended from dinosaurs because the bone structure of Archaeopteryx and Coelurosaurus was similar. But recently found fossils of true birds older than Archaeopteryx show that birds and dinosaurs developed in separate ways, though perhaps from a common ancestor. So it is still not known for sure whether Archaeopteryx was descended from dinosaurs. The oldest creatures known with genuinely birdlike features are called protoaves and lived at the start of the Triassic.

The truly birdlike protoavis lived in the Triassic and is older than Archaeopteryx.

● **To the Parent**

Since its discovery in 1861 the Archaeopteryx has been the subject of debate. One theory says that it was not a bird at all but was a feathered dinosaur. Another says it couldn't even fly but used its wings to catch insects. The foremost characteristic of feathers, however, is that by resistance to the air they make flight possible. For the same reason they would have been inefficient tools for catching prey. Archaeopteryx's wings were almost certainly meant for flying. Birds are characterized by feathers, so it is possible that Archaeopteryx branched off from dinosaurs at some stage and can be considered one of the creatures from which modern birds evolved.

Why Did Dinosaurs Die Out?

ANSWER Millions of years ago dinosaurs and other living creatures suddenly died out. No one knows for certain why that happened. Scientists have different ideas or theories about why this change took place. Here are some of their theories.

Dinosaurs, sea reptiles, flying reptiles, some shellfish and fishes, and other creatures became extinct at the same time.

■ Was it because mammals took over?

All living things must adapt to their changing world if they are to survive. This process is called evolution. Sometimes different creatures compete for things like food. When the warm-blooded mammals came along the dinosaurs might have had to compete with them for food. So the mammals survived, and the dinosaurs became extinct.

Hmm. That's possible. But it doesn't explain why many sea creatures also became extinct.

■ Was an egg-eating mammal the cause?

Certainly some mammals lived on dinosaur eggs, but one group of animals could not drive another to extinction in that way. Besides, once its main source of food was gone, what would the survivor live on? It would die out too. No, this couldn't have been the only cause.

This still doesn't explain why some sea creatures also became extinct!

■ Did dinosaurs starve to death?

That is possible. About the time the dinosaurs died the earth's climate changed. The kinds of plants that dinosaurs ate died and were replaced by different ones. Maybe that's why plant eaters died out. And once they were gone the meat eaters would have no food either, so they would die out too.

But the new plants took time to develop. Why couldn't plant eaters have adapted to eating them instead?

■ Did the cause come from outer space?

Another theory is that something terrible happened in outer space that changed the earth and caused the dinosaurs to die. Or maybe the earth was hit by a big meteor shower or one huge meteor. That could have changed the planet in such a way that the dinosaurs were no longer able to live here.

It would have left a mark on the earth. There is nothing to show that that happened.

■ What about massive volcanic activity?

Some scientists wonder if volcanoes are the reason that the dinosaurs died out. Maybe there was a long period of time when volcanoes kept erupting in different places. If this had happened the volcanoes could have filled the air with so much dust and pollution that animal life would begin to die out. Could this be the explanation?

I don't think any volcanic action occurring after earth was formed could be that bad!

■ Was it a change in climate?

At the same time that the dinosaurs died the earth's climate changed. Now there were hot and cold seasons. Cold-blooded creatures like dinosaurs survive best when the climate is nice and warm. When the weather is cold they become slow moving and sleepy. Dinosaurs may have died out because they could not stand the cold climate.

That's all very well but we still must explain why the climate changed.

No simple answer explains the death of the dinosaurs. We need to explore several theories if we are to find the right answer. Let's turn the page and read more about it.

● To the Parent

Geology classifies the formation of the earth into eras and periods. These then are defined by major evolutionary changes in life that took place within their time frame. The great dying, or wholesale extinction of numerous life forms, that occurred at the end of the Cretaceous is the event separating the Mesozoic and Cenozoic Eras. As well as the dinosaurs, invertebrates like the ammonites, and marine and flying reptiles suddenly disappeared. Why all this happened still puzzles the world's scientists.

Why Did the Earth's Climate Change?

ANSWER It seems that a change in climate could explain the death of the dinosaurs. But what could have caused this change? Scientists who study the earth's minerals think that a giant meteor struck the earth long ago. Here's how that could change the climate.

How could a meteorite cause such a change?

The impact of a meteorite six miles (9.6 km) across would bring extreme climatic changes and destroy many life forms.

Scientists think a giant meteorite may have changed the earth's climate.

The impact sends lots of dust and gas into the atmosphere.

It puts a lid on the earth, and the planet gets extremely hot.

The lid blocks sunlight too, so the climate later gets very cold.

What Climatic Changes Might Have Done

Dinosaurs needed warmth and were affected by the cold, which also destroyed plants. This left them without food.

Dinosaurs, especially the cold-blooded ones, couldn't survive in extremely cold weather.

Cold-blooded reptiles survived by hibernating, and warm-blooded mammals by staying active.

■ Other reasons for the change

Even if a meteorite did not strike the earth we know that the climate changed. Things on earth could have caused this change too. When the land began to form continents giant seas formed. That would probably have made the earth cooler. Or perhaps volcanoes caused the change. If they erupted for a long time they would fill the sky with a cloud of dust. This could block the sun and cool the earth.

Volcanic ash blocking the sun would have the same effect.

Sea water between the continents could have caused it.

● **To the Parent**

Some scientists disagree with the meteorite collision theory because of the absence of dinosaur fossils in the irradiated stratum. Neither does it explain the change in plant life in the late Cretaceous. Five distribution peaks of iridium exist in the earth's strata, and not all indicate collision with a meteorite. Yet arguments for climatic changes are not totally conclusive either.

How Can Fossils Show What Dinosaurs Looked Like?

ANSWER Scientists who study fossils must act like detectives. They use clues to figure out things about dinosaurs. Bones are clues to a dinosaur's size and shape. Teeth tell us what the animal ate. Some fossils provide other clues too.

Fossils are dug out of rocks and the ground.

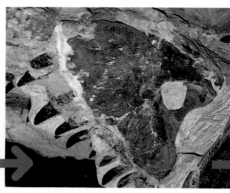

▲ Rocks are removed in one piece to prevent damage to fossils.

▲ This is a fossil of dinosaur skin.

■ Putting it together

Many different kinds of materials go into making pictures and three-dimensional models of dinosaurs.

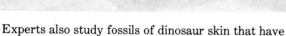

Experts also study fossils of dinosaur skin that have been found. Skin fossils are rarer than bone fossils.

By studying animals living now that resemble dinosaurs, scientists get their ideas about how dinosaurs lived.

No one knows the true color of dinosaurs. Scientists believe that they had coloring like modern reptiles.

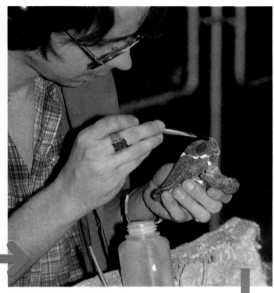

▲ Rocks containing fossils are taken back to the laboratory where special tools are used to remove excess rock and soil carefully.

▲ A special hardening compound is used to protect the fossils.

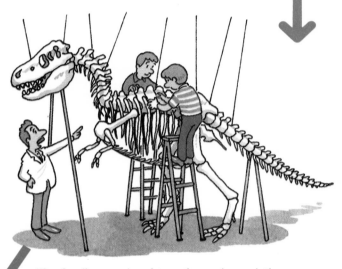

The fossils are pieced together using existing information about body shape for new species.

▲ This is a model of a meat eater.

Based on what is known of the anatomy of animals today, clay muscles are fitted onto a model of the skeleton.

● **To the Parent**

Many different materials and much information are considered in reconstruction of dinosaurs. The evidence of musculature from fossils is compared with that of living creatures. Their posture is determined by the shape of joints. The strata where the fossils were discovered are studied for evidence of environment, which helps in the determination of the creature's life style. Though coloration is never preserved in fossil form the type of environment might be guessed at. And reference to living creatures is a necessary help. Perfecting a reconstruction of a dinosaur always demands a great deal of time, effort and expertise.

? What Are These Fossils?

■ The skull of Tyrannosaurus

Tyrannosaurus, the largest meat eater, had a head that was three feet (91 cm) long.

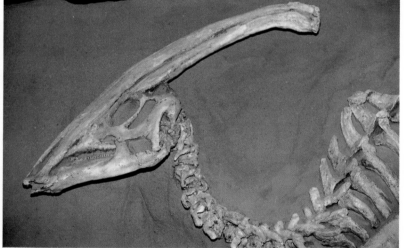

■ Parasaurolophus skull

Its head crest measured 3.3 feet (1 m) long from behind its head to the tip.

■ Skeleton of Corythosaurus

Its head crest was hollow, and it may have been used to make sounds similar to those of a trombone.

■ Fossilized skull of an adult male Lambeosaurus with head crest

Lambeosaurus had a crest at an angle from the front to the back of its head. A male's crest was more exotic than the female's. Crests were fully formed at adulthood and continued to grow.

This skull of a young male does not show the crest. ▶

■ Skeleton of Stegosaurus

Stegosaurus is famous for the bony plates on its back and spikes at the end of its tail.

■ Skeleton of Triceratops

A well-protected and very powerful plant eater, it had two horns on its head and another on its snout.

• To the Parent

Dinosaur fossils are rarely complete when they are found. A total skeleton is usually a composite pieced together from separate finds. A single complete skeleton, if it is discovered, is therefore a rare and priceless treasure.

❓ And What Fossils Do We Have Here?

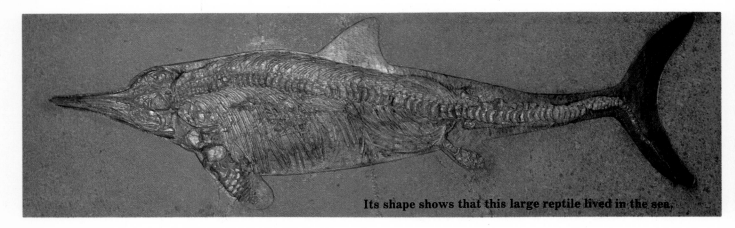

Its shape shows that this large reptile lived in the sea.

■ Skeleton of Ichthyosaurus

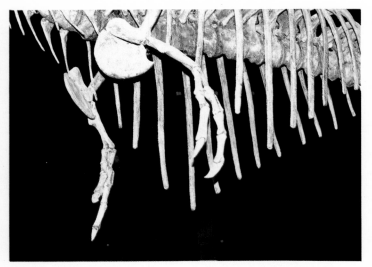

■ Forelegs of Tyrannosaurus

A fossilized skeleton shows meat-eating Tyrannosaurus' tiny two-fingered forelegs.

■ Neck bones of Camarasaurus

The large opening in the skull of this long-necked dinosaur was a blowhole or nostril for breathing.

● **To the Parent**

Dinosaur fossils are usually quite fragile. Because of that dinosaur skeletons on display in museums are mostly replicas modeled on the actual skeletons. The models are finished with special materials so that they look real.

Growing-Up Album

What's Wrong With These Pictures?

There are seven creatures pictured here. If you look at them closely you will find something wrong with each of them. Can you tell what is wrong? Try to guess before looking at the answers at the bottom of the page.

Tyrannosaurus

Apatosaurus

No armor for Tyrannosaurus or feathers for Pteranodon. Apatosaurus has lost its tail, and Triceratops has too many horns.

82

Pteranodon

Parasaurolophus

Triceratops

Elasmosaurus

Ichthyosaurus

The fins on Ichthyosaurus and the mouth on Parasaurolophus are wrong. Elasmosaurus was a creature with flippers, not legs.

Can You Match These Up?

Some of the creatures shown in silhouette lived in water and some on land. The body positions of the silhouettes are different from the pictures below. Can you match them?

■ Match the pictures

Ancient reptiles came in many shapes and sizes. See if you can match the ones at the right with the shapes on the top part of the page.

Pteranodon

Elasmosaurus

Triceratops

1. Apatosaurus 2. Triceratops 3. Stegosaurus 4. Tyrannosaurus 5. Pteranodon

Apatosaurus

Mosasaurus

Stegosaurus

Tyrannosaurus

Ichthyosaurus

6. Elasmosaurus 7. Ichthyosaurus 8. Mosasaurus

Who Is Speaking?

Ten prehistoric creatures are shown on these two pages, and each of them is saying something. Can you match what is being said with the creature saying it? Remember what you have learned about dinosaurs from reading this book.

① On my hind legs I have huge claws that I use as weapons. I can tuck them in when I'm running or whip them out quickly if an enemy should attack me.

Stegosaurus

Tyrannosaurus

Pteranodon

Parasaurolophus

Baryonyx

⑤ I'm the most ferocious, largest meat eater that ever lived. I'm huge, but my two-fingered forelimbs are tiny compared with the rest of my body.

⑥ You can tell from my wings that I fly, but I'm not a bird. Not me! I am covered with hair, and I have a noticeable head crest.

⑦ I walk erect and have a horn on my nose. I got my name because I love eggs. Other creatures' eggs! I steal them when the owners aren't looking!

1. I'm Deinonychus. 2. I'm Parasaurolophus. 3. I'm Baryonyx. 4. I'm Mosasaurus . 5. Tyrannosaurus, that's me!

② I eat plants and have a hollow crest on my head. I'm nicknamed "trombone" because I probably used my crest like a trombone to make noises with.

③ I'm a land dweller, but on my front legs I have huge claws, which I use for catching fish. You can be sure that I don't eat plants.

④ I'm a kind of crocodile. I have fins instead of legs and live in the sea, not the river. I eat fish and ammonites. I even eat a pterosaur or two.

Elasmosaurus

Ichthyosaurus

Oviraptor

Deinonychus

Mosasaurus

⑧ I live in the sea, look like a dolphin and swim like one. Though I'm a reptile, not a mammal, I don't lay eggs. I give birth to live young.

⑨ I have a long neck. I live in the sea and eat fish. I sometimes catch pterosaurs out of the air too. But I'm afraid of sharks.

⑩ I am a plant eater with my own special armor. The plates down my back keep my body heat just right and protect me. My spiked tail is a deadly weapon.

6. I'm Pteranodon. 7. I'm Oviraptor. 8. I'm Ichthyosaurus. 9. I'm Elasmosaurus. 10. And I'm Stegosaurus. Bet you guessed!

A Child's First Library of Learning

Dinosaurs

Time-Life Books Inc. is a wholly owned subsidiary of
Time Incorporated.
Time-Life Books, Alexandria, Virginia
Children's Publishing

Publisher:	Robert H. Smith
Editorial Director:	Neil Kagan
Associate Editor:	Jean Burke Crawford
Marketing Director:	Ruth P. Stevens
Promotion Director:	Kathleen B. Tresnak
Associate Promotion Director:	Jane B. Welihozkiy
Production Manager:	Prudence G. Harris
Editorial Consultants:	Jacqueline A. Ball
	Andrew Gutelle

Editorial Supervision by:
International Editorial Services Inc.
Tokyo, Japan

Editor:	C. E. Berry
Associate Editor:	Winston S. Priest
Translation:	Joseph Hlebica
	Bryan Harrell
Writer:	Pauline Bush
Editorial Staff:	Christine Alaimo
	Nobuko Abe

Cover: © 1989 Mark Hallett

TIME LIFE ®

Library of Congress Cataloging in Publication Data
Dinosaurs.
 p. cm.—(A Child's first library of learning)
 Summary: Questions and answers provide information
about the behavior and possible fate of dinosaurs. Includes
charts, diagrams, and an activities section.
 ISBN 0-8094-4889-0. ISBN 0-8094-4890-4 (lib. bdg.)
 1. Dinosaurs—Juvenile literature. [1. Dinosaurs—
Miscellanea. 2. Questions and answers.]
I. Time-Life Books. II. Series.
QE862.D5D516 1989 567.9'1—dc20 89-4532
©1989 Time-Life Books Inc.
©1983 Gakken Co. Ltd.

All rights reserved. No part of this book may be reproduced in
any form or by any electronic or mechanical means, including
information storage and retrieval devices or systems, without
prior written permission from the publisher, except that brief
passages may be quoted for review.

Second printing 1991. Printed in U.S.A.
Published simultaneously in Canada.

TIME-LIFE is a trademark of Time Warner Inc. U.S.A.

Time-Life Books Inc. offers a wide range of fine publications,
including home video products. For subscription information, call
1-800-621-7026 or write TIME-LIFE BOOKS, P.O. Box C-32068,
Richmond, Virginia 23261-2068.